God ever whisper

Edwina

Whispers

Conversations with Edwina Gateley

Edwina Gateley
and
Jane Hammond-Clarke

SOURCE BOOKS • TRABUCO CANYON CALIFORNIA

First edition, June 2000

Library of Congress Cataloging-in-Publication Data

Gateley, Edwina.

Whispers: conversations with Edwina Gateley / Edwina
Gateley and Jane Hammond-Clarke.--1st ed.

p. cm.

ISBN 0-940147-50-5 (trade pbk.)

1. Spiritual Life--Catholic Church. I Hammond-Clarke,
Jane, 1956- II. Title.

BX2350.65 .G37 2000

242--dc21   00-036546

ISBN: 0-940147-50-5

Source Books
P.O. Box 794
Trabuco Canyon CA 92678

Printed and bound in the USA by KNI, Anaheim CA

Contents

Foreword

EDWINA GATELEY HAS MADE HER WORLD and our world a better place. She goes to the edges and crosses boundaries that keep most of us in our well-contained cubicles. We are often afraid to push the limits of our lives, but Edwina, who is shown in these conversations to be an ordinary human being attempting the extraordinary, can be an inspiration to us as she breaks loose from conventions.

Before I met Edwina, I had edited audiotapes of her talks. Her booming voice and life-changing stories made me envision a six-foot tall, strapping, burly woman who could hold her own on the streets. I was most surprised when this petite woman was introduced to me.

Over the years Edwina has become like family, and we have spent many an evening sharing a glass of wine or a cup of tea. One night, sitting on a green sofa in my California home, our conversation became so intense that the idea for this book was born. I flew to Pennsylvania to spend a week with Edwina and her family and we spent hours at her cabin recording our conversations. As portrait photography is my profession, I took photographs of Edwina and her son to accompany her themes.

There are also three photographs of my husband, taken in the Mojave Desert. I thought it appropriate to include representation of an adult male. Without Denis' editing of the rough transcripts of the conversations, this book would not have come to fruit.

Edwina has taught me that we have a great many opportunities to let God work in our lives, and that even the smallest kindness can make a huge difference in the world.

JHC

Breathing
in
God

Persistent God

Persistent God!
What is it with you
that you are ever
hovering near,
unseen presence
like the air
we breathe - so unthinkingly?

Persistent God!
What is it with you,
that you so believe
we can become
as angels
shimmering with holy grace
and powerful tenderness?

Persistent God!
What is it with you
that still,
against all our small dark doings
you wait around
in ridiculous longing
to raise us
to the stars?

Persistent God!
Persistent God!
What is it with you
that you never cease
to be suffused
with great hot desire
to scoop us up
and love us?

I HAVE A TINY WOODEN CABIN here in the corner of this Benedictine property. It is like a little hidden womb for me to escape to now and then.

Most people's lives are absolutely filled from the moment they wake up until the time they go to bed. They are exhausted. People are exhausted! Everybody I meet says "I've got this to do or that to do." There is so much information coming in, there is so much work people have to do, there are so many problems people have to cope with. Our lives are saturated with activities and things, with personal concerns, not to mention anxieties about the world and the planet.

How do we stay tuned into the deep God space within us? We do have to take some practical steps. We do have to have a red light which shines out at a certain point, saying, Stop! We need to stop in our tracks and take a breath, a breath of God.

I don't mean that we have to go away for a week, a month or three months to a desert retreat. I mean that we have to practice breathing God into our hectic schedules. Maybe we are conscious of the need to take five minutes in our morning or afternoon routines or at the end of the day when we sit down, and instead of putting on the television or calling somebody to chat or going out for a drink, we might just sit quietly in a favorite place to be with God.

The Mystics and the Sufis of Eastern wisdom say that God is the very breath we breathe. The Hebrew word for the Holy Spirit is *ruah* which means breath, and all of us have access to breath. It is not expensive, we don't pay for it and it is not rationed.

We *can* breathe God into our souls. We have just forgotten how to do it, or we haven't been taught to do it in the first place. What we have been taught is to talk *out* to God. If we could get into a rhythm of spirituality where we save a little space for God each day and become aware that we are breathing in God, we would have a greater sense of meaning in our lives.

Without breath we die. When we breathe in deeply we nourish the God presence within us, we calm ourselves. And it is a simple thing to do. The way to wholeness and holiness is not necessarily an agonizing descent into the interior life, nor a tortuous ascent up Jacob's ladder. Rather, it is, for the most part, the simple practice of being open to God. We can do it in the train, at the traffic lights, we can do it in the office, on the coffee-break. We do not need books, bells, candles, semesters in college, credit or a checkbook. We need only breathe with awareness. After a little while it can become a way of life.

Most of us are panting, we are gasping for breath as we rush to the next task on the list. We are too busy to be aware that we are missing out. God is unable to enter us deeply because we don't let God in. And yet God wants to fill us completely.

So I am blessed to have this little cabin, a womb where I am reminded constantly that I can breathe in God. I am fortunate. Not everyone can run away to a cabin in the woods. It is here for those few occasions when I am not looking after my child or travelling around giving retreats and conferences. I don't deny that in an airplane or in a restaurant I have as much access to God as I have in this hermitage—it's just that the peaceful environment here is much more conducive to breathing and relaxing.

Of course God is not particular. God doesn't need roses and waves and wind gently blowing in order to be present within us. God is quite happy with airport announcements and trains, God is really okay with all that stuff. It is *we* who are picky and needy. So we seek out spaces where we can listen to the waves, and the wind, and I think God is content with that. God knows that *we* are limited and that we need special effects and environments!

God is happy with anywhere. You can be up a tree, for heaven's sake. We don't need to limit God by saying we can only be with God at certain times or in certain places. If that were the case, then what about the millions of people who live in poverty? They would not have access to God because they could not afford a hermitage, or a retreat, or spiritual guidance. Do you think God would have created a way to be spiritual that depended on your pocket book? No. God is saying, 'I am in all places.'

On the other hand, because we are needy, it is good for us to try and make a holy place in our surroundings. Who is spiritually mature enough to be able to readily experience God in the hustle and bustle of ordinary life? We have to create pockets. The time must come when we don't need little pockets of beauty in order to experience God. This cabin hermitage is like a novitiate, a stepping-stone— it helps, but eventually, if I gain spiritual maturity, I must leave the cabin behind and find that space in my heart. We have to leave the hermitage, leave the mountain top, leave the retreat centers and know that God travels with us wherever we are.

In the meantime, everybody should have access to a special place that reminds them they can breathe in God.

I bring the women of Genesis House here. These are women who are victims of prostitution, drugs, institutionalized abuse, and they need to gather in a place where they can be away from the inner city with all its noise and demands. Such people have as much right to beauty as those who can pay for these special places and experiences. I am not happy with the way that the religious and the secular are separated. All of us deserve access to sacred spaces. If we are to be truly spiritual we must break down the barriers and provide places of silence, tranquility and beauty for street people and women recovering from prostitution, as well as for we who are privileged.

This cabin is a reminder. When I bring the women here they gasp at how lovely it is, and I ask them to remember it when they go back to the city streets, to remember that God is as much in the squalid city as in the woods by a lake. That is hard for them. That is hard for anybody!

There is no doubt that we can see God more clearly in beauty and in sunrises. But spiritually mature people do not depend on special places. The special times and places are as nurturing as a mother providing milk for her child. God nurtures us to remind us of God's presence. But God depends on nothing, no particular environment. God *is*.

I love this place. In truth I need it to remind me that I am spiritually immature and need a bit of help. I am grateful for it, and when I leave here after a few hours or days I hope I am able to go out into the world and do my stuff with a little more awareness, having been in touch with the silence in my soul.

The interesting thing is that we always have access to new beginnings until the day we die. You can be sixty or a hundred, and be hungry for spirituality and for God and start seeking right from where you are. The spiritual path is not dependent on age any more than it is dependent on where you are. God transcends everything.

§

The Breathing in God that is called prayer is simply *awareness*. It does not require special techniques, we can all do it. One way to pray is to still the body, to be quiet, to breathe deeply and to enter into being aware of your own body. We need to breathe deeply and to become conscious, in a moment's silence, of God entering into us and nourishing us in the pits of our being.

Because I want to become a whole person and to go deeper than I am and be more aware of God, I have to try to carve out ten, twenty or thirty minutes a day to breathe in and sit with God. I am not always able to do it, but I keep trying to give half an hour of the sixteen or eighteen that I am awake, to breathe in God.

To take half an hour of conscious Godness is to nurture myself. When I don't manage it, it doesn't mean that God is absent, it only means that I have lost communication with the Godness deep inside myself.

§

All of us need to be aware of being with God at certain points. We have seen that it does not need to be in a special place, but it should be a place where we can feel totally alone where we can enter into our own solitude.

It's like being in the bathroom. When we are in the bathroom we are alone, we give our selves to the experience of going to the bathroom. And we don't think about saying "I don't have time to go to the bathroom, I have a busy life you know." We know our body's physical needs. If we were as conscious of our spiritual needs as we are of our bodily needs, be it eating, or having a cup of coffee, we would be in far better spiritual health. We must remember that the spiritual life is as important as the physical life.

We will never be healthy unless we integrate the spiritual, physical and psychological aspects of our being. Just as we feed the body and deal with the needs of the body, we must also feed God and deal with our need for God.

Somehow we have separated our spirituality from the rest of our being. We must not distinguish between spiritual, mental and physical health. The separation is artificial and unholy. We must put the three together and then we can start to talk about healing, holiness, wholeness. Only then will we understand that God is in all of our being not just in the place we call 'soul.'

We wish we were able to buy spirituality just as we buy food for the table or pay for a course of study, but breathing God is something we must do for ourselves. It is a very simple thing. We would never dream of saying that we are too busy to eat or sleep. We know we would die without eating or sleeping. And spiritually we are dying—many of us are spiritually dead. People say, "I don't know if I can find ten minutes to pray." We have to do certain things to keep alive and functioning properly. In recognizing the need for our wholeness and our wellness we must adjust our priorities and give each its due.

People who do not look after their emotional life end up in therapy. With our spiritual life it is the same— except there are few doctors. We are not used to taking care of ourselves, we always want to go to someone whom we think knows more. But ultimately no-one can heal us except ourselves.

This is the generation of the experts. There are experts everywhere: psychobabblers and psycho-what-nots. We have made ourselves dependent on them. When we are told we must be our own expert we panic. We say, "I don't know anything." But that is fine, we don't need to know anything. We simply need to take responsibility for our own spiritual health.

Women especially are inclined to consult others about their inner life. They can come to depend on their spiritual directors, and I have heard some talk as if it is *the thing* to have a spiritual director. A spiritual director is most appropriate for when we are at a crossroads, for when we are spiritually lost and need someone to point the way forward. But if the help becomes a crutch and we cannot walk without it, independent growth can be hindered.

Here we are in the most wealthy nation in the world and we want to pay for God. But no matter how many of those books on one or another aspect of spirituality appear in the bookstores, people will still be spiritually hungry unless they are converted deep down and let go of the crutches and all the clutter. In putting this book together we are offering only a guide. But when we really have reached where we should be as a people called to wholeness, books such as this will not be necessary, our spiritual life will be centered deep *inside*. We will reflect God's face, we will create the Realm of God on Earth.

For humankind to be whole and spiritual, the time must come when people can be hermits and mystics and everyone will know that they are an important part of society rather than fringe folk. In the global village there will be many shamans, warriors and prophets. But at present, in our dominant and dominating secular western culture there is no place for the holy. A time must come when we who participate in this culture, make up this society, learn to breathe in God and make ourselves whole. When this time comes, mystical awareness will be a normal (not extraordinary) part of life.

Beginnings

Beginnings

Beginnings –
just tiny stirrings
which disturb our even surface,
prodding us into new and different shapes...
claiming their place
on our horizons –
stretching us
where we would not go –
yet we must.
Driven by life forces
deeper than our dreams,
we dare to rise
and grasp towards
the new young thing –
not yet born –
but insistent –
like a tight seed bursting
for life,
carrying within it
all the power
of a woman's
birthing thrust.

I WAS NOT RAISED WITH GOD as central in my life. We were not very religious, the people in my family were not avid churchgoers. I stumbled across God as I was growing up—a teenager experiencing problems at school, wanting to be accepted and so on. Church was not a significant part of my life until I began to run into the basic human conditions of loneliness, the need for acceptance and struggles at home. Then God became my refuge.

I think I hooked onto God as my friend, my solace, and that is okay: we are human and we use God. God becomes the comforter, the secret friend, the conspirator. So God filled a space in my life. Believe it or not, I was a very withdrawn, shy child, and when I stumbled on God it appeared that God had no expectations of me. God simply *was*. God was God . God was my big friend in the sky to whom I could talk at anytime without an invitation.

In my city we had a cathedral, big and old, always dark inside and smelling of incense and candle wax. It became for me a secret garden, my haven, the place to which I escaped. From the age of twelve I would go into that cathedral as though I were going into a great womb and I would be comforted by the biggest, best friend I could ever know. I would sit there for hours, learning to contemplate without knowing what I was doing, simply by being there in the darkness and smelling the incense and the candles. I knew I was experiencing deep within me something that was tangible, that this being with God would affect me physically. I felt God's presence, and I came to treasure it.

And so God and I became partners in my teenage years, so much so that I could not imagine a life separate from God even though as I began to grow, my awareness, my images of God changed. In the beginning I made deals with God as you do with friends—you give me this and I'll give you that, let's swap and trade. So I would say to God, "You let me do well on my school exams and let me get to college and I'll become a missionary."

And we all do that. In this first stage of our spiritual journey God is someone with whom we can negotiate, like a big Daddy in the sky. We get presents from him and if we are naughty we will be punished in one way or another. In the Catholic tradition, we responded with guilt and confession, and were forgiven.

So that was the God of my early years. When we are young we cannot see God as being within us. We start with a God outside, and God takes us to where we are now. It doesn't matter to God where we start. What matters is that we are there and we are listening and we want a relationship.

As I grew older, God became bigger. I began to run into problems and struggles in my mission work, and there were times when it was as if God were absent. I was not prepared for an absent God, I was used to God being present all the time.

God was present to the child, but as I grew up that God became elusive. This is where we have to stretch. When we truly have a relationship and truly love, it is not going to be one big jolly relationship. There are going to be heights and depths and plateaus and we must accept that and grow with it.

So, there were times when I wondered why God was not there anymore. And that is when I had to determine if because I could not experience God, did it mean there *was* no God? Or would my faith stretch me and carry me through to an ongoing, maturing relationship with God?

I think it is at that point that a lot of people give up, and let God die. We can call this the Abandonment Experience or the Dark Night, but it is inevitable in any healthy relationship. No relationship is constant, and so it is with God. Yet it is possible to see a way through, and to continue to be faithful to a relationship that is no longer as it was. Being faithful does not mean simply feeling good, though that is what most of us want. We want to feel God. We want to feel warm and fuzzy, but that is not the way a relationship deepens nor how wisdom comes. We have to learn to hold on to *nothing*. It is the little bit of faith and the little bit of light, the seed that carries us past the point of intellectually knowing that God is with us, even when we cannot see. It is knowing God is there when we can't feel God. It is knowing God loves us when we don't feel loved. It is a necessary part of the spiritual journey.

This is reflected in an experience I had when I went to stay in a hermitage for a few months. I wrote a poem and put it on the door of the old trailer in the woods. The words came right from my soul—I know that because I didn't know what I was writing until I had finished. Sometimes people get inspirations and say, "Oh, did *I* say that? Did *I* write that?" And the words were,

> *When I asked my God if I could come and*
> *stay with him awhile, she replied—Yes but*
> *don't bring your god with you.*

We all have images of God that change as we develop and grow spiritually and sooner or later these gods have to die. Ultimately the big Daddy god in the sky, the big magic god who will perform tricks for us and work miracles for us, and the god who will sort out all our problems and win us the lottery—these gods have to die, and we have to let go of those images to allow God to be in us. The true God. No performer no magician, no big brother, but God who is all things and no things, who simply *is*. And that is the mystical experience. God has to die and our gods and icons have to die until we are left with nothing but an awareness that God holds us right in the middle of the nothing.

§

That is the Dark Night of the Soul, the emptying. We try to fit God into a box because of our superficial needs and because we have a penchant for control. We expect that God is something like a human person with a big bag of tricks and goodies to hand out if we behave ourselves.

But God breaks out of all those boundaries. I don't think we have a notion of how big God is. Our little god will shatter as we get on with our lives. The little images we have of daddy and magician will shatter as we grow in wisdom and understand that God is beyond all our images.

We will never be able to fully understand God until we come face to face with God. The mystics know that we must sink into God, that we must sink into that deep empty space within us, and sit with it. And God brings a deep peace so that we flow with God. We go through life much more deeply and peacefully flowing with whatever

19
—

happens in the shadows, the darkness, the heights, the depths, the struggles, knowing that God holds us in the palm of God's hand.

If we can imagine God holding us, a speck in God's hand, it brings about a deep peace and an awareness that God is actually in control. We don't need to control God or to persuade God to do this or that, God is way ahead of us and knows our actions and thoughts, even before we do.

Spiritual maturity involves a process of letting-go rather than adding-on or acquiring. In some ways, ironically, it is a negative rather than a positive. We begin to allow God to flow through our lives rather than trying to manage God.

§

In the course of my travels, I come across many old people, some 'shut-ins', and when I talk with them about ministry or working with the homeless they say, "I can't do anything now. I wish I were younger." I tell them that probably they can do more than others, because the activities of ministry are only a prelude to experiencing God in the wisdom of old age, where we sit with God rather than scurry around trying to *do* things for God. Old people have great potential to be mystics. They have the opportunity to *be* with God and to be Zen masters or Christian mystics, while the rest of us run around saying, "I haven't got time to be with God, I haven't got time to listen to God because I'm working with the poor and the homeless."

Those old or invalided or sick people who think their time is over and that they have no more to contribute, can give an incredible amount to a world which is hungry for depth and hungry for prayer and hungry for the mystical.

They should be the ones who are our spiritual teachers and gurus instead of feeling, as we have made them feel, 'Well now you're sick or old, you can't do anything.' Let us learn from them. We do too much, we must stop *doing* and begin *being* and allow ourselves to be soaked in God rather than running around all the time, trying to save the world. Let us honor *sitting*.

In the Book of Isaiah it says,
In your old age I shall still be the same, when your hair is grey I shall still support you.

Isaiah 46:4 JB

It is beautiful that God considers old age an invitation rather than a barrier to becoming holy and becoming a saint. In fact, as we enter old age we have gone through so much that we have a deeper sense of God if only we have allowed our false images of God to die. We see this in some people who are at death's door. They begin to accept that life is over but they don't go crazy, instead they begin to experience a deep peace. They say, " Hey, God can take over." It is an extraordinary conversion experience when we are able to say that, when we allow God to take over our lives.

Just think how peaceful we would become if we were to allow God to take over our lives when we are young rather than when we are death's door. When we have a problem or a crisis is when we find we *can* give ourselves over to God, rather than trying to take care of the problems alone. We have to stop and say, "God, hold us in the palm of your hand."

There is a fine line between totally accepting God in our times of trouble, saying, "Take over, I can't handle things any more, you're in charge," and being angry and completely letting go of God. I think it is a moment of grace that takes us one way or the other. But if we are accustomed to being open to God's grace, then we are more likely to let God take over.

I think it is when we are still children, still spiritual infants, that we expect God to take care of our lives and to fix everything, like the divine Mr. Fixit. As spiritual children, we think that when things are not fixed it is because our faith is not deep enough. It is childlike not to realize that God is there in the disasters and the crises as well as in the joys and the celebrations. We don't have maturity of faith.

That is why there are a lot of people who cannot handle God. They say, "Why does God let this bad thing happen? Why didn't God save my mother? Why did my child get sick?" Their image of God as the divine magician has been shattered. At that point is the invitation to conversion where people can find a God who may not be magical but who loves us passionately. We either have to trust in the process of living and dying and death and new life, or we expect instant results and consolations. The god of instant results and satisfaction is a false god.

I think through much of our lives we worship a false god, and we have given that god fancy names. Since everyone else seems to be worshiping false gods it seems reasonable to do likewise. But ultimately, if we are open, God will indeed allow our lives to be shattered so that we can be invited to a deeper faith.

We try to anticipate God all the time. We think that if we are going to have a relationship with God it might well mean a thunderball dropping on our heads, or receiving a blinding revelation at any time. God does not dispense joys and pains like a capricious being enjoying a power trip. God does not go around dispensing traumas. They are part and parcel of who we are, part and parcel of being human. God is with us in those events, but God does not give them to us or cause them. God does not walk around saying "I am going to clobber you now." That is a false image of God. God is not capricious. God is love.

§

We never fully know or possess God, we never fully become a reflection of God. We are always *en route,* on the journey, and we are so desperate to get along the road that we look at people who are in a different place and we say, "Look where they are! There it is. That's it!"

These are false leads. All of us are in the place we are supposed to be. In God's good time we grow and move on and continue the journey.

And certainly I am aware that I am not the full person I am called to be, I am still struggling with entering into God's presence in my own life. It's never an easy journey. We are forever on the way. My image of God is changing even now. Right up to now, I still hold onto my external God because this image allows me to talk with God as with a human being. But what I am struggling to know is that I don't so much need to *talk* to God as to sink into God deep within me, and be aware of God's presence. We don't need the great long conversation, such things are preliminaries—I know this, but it is a struggle for me to listen because I am so used to talking to God.

He, and I mean, *she* and I have great conversations. My God has moved from a he to a she and now to a nothing. God is not he-god, is not she-god is not I don't-know-what. God is not finished, finite. I don't have answers to the mystery of what God is, I know only that there is a God, something bigger than me. I used to talk to it. But now I think am I talking to myself. I used to listen to it, but now I think I am listening to myself.

And now I think that is alright. Now I have to accept that God *is,* and God is in me. And that I am a reflection of God. But I have not entered into that reality because it is at the same time much simpler and more complex than having a good and divine pal, up there, outside, to whom I can keep chatting. The more I talk, the less I listen. I think the more we pursue the spiritual journey, the more we become silent. We might have a greater chance of hearing God's whisper in our hearts if we talk less.

But silence is a difficult process: the whispering God is harder to get hold of than the familiar God in the sky to whom I can talk all the time, saying what I want and what I feel and what I desire. And if I stop talking, what do I do then? How do I quiet the mind? How do I quiet my thoughts and images so I can simply sink into a deep awareness of God?

So, this is a relationship which deepens and darkens as we grow spiritually. The deeper and darker one goes the more one knows almost nothing. It becomes harder to be certain of anything as one begins to enter into God in our world, God in ourselves.

There are no more certainties, so we need to stop preaching. But we are a nation of preachers. We stand up and say, "God wants this, God says that, God expects the other. Let us do this for God." All this is infant spirituality. We must shut up.

We shut up when we realize that all God wants us to do is say "Yes," and to *be* love. We don't need to preach when we are lovers. We simply are. Anybody who has been in love knows that. It is perfectly good to simply sit and look at one's lover. But when we start chittering and chattering, the quality of the relationship starts changing. The deepest relationship is one in which we can hold hands and simply gaze at one another. This is love, and so it is with God. When we stop demanding presents and we stop talking all the time, and we begin to move into *being with,* instead of demanding, there is a deepening of our spirituality. And I know now that it can well be presumptuous and arrogant to stand and preach to people about who God is and what they should be doing for God, because the relationship of each person with God is unique.

My relationship and my journey with God is not going to be yours, and that is beautiful. Each of us walks on a parallel path, but God relates to each of us differently, uniquely. So, I must look at you with wonder and say that wherever you are is the right place. Wherever I am is the right place for me. God unfolds in us, God *becomes* in us. At what point is a rose a rose? The seed? The bud? The flower? It is all rose. I cannot preach to you about what you need to do, and you do not look at me and say, "She's there, she's got it." It does not matter. We must be where we are.

The more I think I have 'It', God, the less I have. In this, Zen & Christian mysticism move together. As in Zen, for instance, entering the mystery involves letting go and allowing no-thing to take over. Institutionalized Christianity, however, has lumbered itself with rules and requirements for undertaking the journey into the mystery, and has made it extremely complicated and often misleading. We get stuck in adhering to the rules, and lose the spontaneity of stepping forward.

I think there is a difference between the feminine and the masculine approaches here. We have created a masculine way of pursuing the spiritual journey: there is the goal, this is the way, and these are the steps you take to get there. The feminine journey is a circling, falling, a mystery and a shadow experience. And that is what we have neglected in Christianity. Now it is being rediscovered through the mystics and through a spiritual hunger which people in this generation are feeling very deeply.

The church was organized by men and therefore it reflected the image of the male, of the patriarchal conqueror-magician. God became the ideal warrior king. But there is no king. Nor is there a queen. God is love.

§

People talk about prayer and often find the easiest way to pray is through speech. Fair enough, that but that is not going to lead us into any depth. In the mystical tradition we stop talking and we are silent. We experience solitude, and it is hard for us because it means we have to relinquish some control. And we are constantly assailed by the ego: what's happening in my life? What happened yesterday? What am I going to have for dinner? These are all distractions of the ego, wanting to keep us busy.

We resist meditative and contemplative prayer because we don't know how to deal with letting go. The struggle is to *be,* not to speak. The struggle for us is to be expectant. We think, "If I don't talk, will God hear me?" Maybe it is more a matter of, "If I don't *listen* will I hear God?"

A natural setting helps us to contemplate because it stills us, it allows us to touch our essential nature and is conducive to silence. We carve out bits of time and go on holy retreats and think that is the magic answer— two days in the woods is the prescription. But ultimately we have to be active contemplatives, we have to be working employees, filled with God's grace. We have to bring the sacred into the workplace, the mall, the streets. We have to *be* the sacred and reflect the sacred ourselves, rather than escaping to find it. We have to allow the sacred to surface in our lives so that we become reflections of God's presence wherever we are. That is how we sanctify the world: by being God's presence in the world. We need to learn how to do that.

Prayer

Stillpoint

Contemplation happens when,
seduced by longing,
we let go our grasp
of our well-constructed
temples of defence and security
abandoning ourselves –
all naked and unknowing –
to the pursuit
of the hunger in our guts.
Ah, then,
when all our bright masks
are left aside,
we fall into
ourselves,
perhaps to meet there,
all cradled by emptiness –
the Stillpoint
rooting us in divinity
and washing us over
in deep, deep peace.

PRAYER IS MUCH SIMPLER than people make it out to be. We have inherited traditions and ritual which tell us to stand or sit or kneel, fold our hands, bow our heads when we are in holy places.

But we have cheated God and we have cheated our experience of God by limiting prayer to particular forms. What is happening now in this generation is that people have realized how hungry we are for a God who is much bigger than the small space we give to God in our holy places and in the time allotted to prayer.

Many people are no longer going to a church to pray because they are finding it does not necessarily lead them to prayer, it does not have the meaning for them that it did in the past when people passively accepted the forms and formulas of how to pray and worship. I think God has escaped from our definitions, and we are experiencing now that prayer grows with us. We grow into prayer as we grow in wisdom, as we become more aware that God cannot, will not be limited to any particular human experience or any single human event. God escapes, and we begin to experience God as life-sized—far bigger that the tiny god we put in a box as we were growing up. When people leave Church, they don't leave God. God always comes along—even if they don't know it.

But now people are saying, "Where is the new God?" And once again we make the mistakes of the past. If we don't find God in church, we seek out the experts to tell us where to find God. What we have to do instead is trust in our personal experience, trust that God is to be found in our every breath, our every motion, our natural life cycles.

In other words, God is far more expansive than our minds are able to grasp. God is already soaked in everything. When something is soaked, when water is soaked in a sponge, you cannot say, "Show me where the water is in this sponge." The answer has to be found on a deeper level. The sponge is saturated with the water as we are saturated with God.

We are out of touch with that awareness because we dare not imagine that God loves so much. So we partition God. For instance, we know that 'Jesus is God's Son.' But we go on to declare that Jesus is 'God's *only* Son.' Biblically, we are all called to be the Children of God. Jesus was the *first* one to live fully his awareness and openness to God. Jesus is the model of God's child. We are all to be models. We are all to be God's children.

And if we look at the life of Jesus and see how he was filled with wonder, how he talked about the lilies of the field, the birds of the air, how God counts every hair of our head, that blows your mind. I mean, how many hairs do you have on your head anyway? Meditate on the hairs of your head instead of on some picture on a wall, actually personalize the thought, and begin to imagine that God is conscious of every single hair on your head (and knows when one falls out)! That is enough material for us to begin to understand how God is thoroughly soaked in our reality! The divine is extremely close to us, yet we have separated the divine from the human.

We have inherited the belief that humanity and the Earth are far away from God, and we have to reach *out* to God, separate ourselves from being human so that we might be holy. And that notion has separated us from an awareness of God being soaked in who we are.

Our task now is to move our eyes from Heaven down to Earth, to move our eyes from statues and icons and to look at ourselves. And to begin to count the hairs on our heads. And to remember that God is in every single hair on our heads.

Maybe we are not wise enough to be able to move Heaven down to Earth yet. We don't trust enough or believe enough to do that. We want a distant God, we want a God 'up there,' far away from us, whom we can talk at. It takes maturity and spiritual wisdom and humility to do otherwise. I think we feel the need to hook onto a God outside us because we do not trust or embrace the wonder of our own humanity. We cannot believe that God is so intimate and close to us, that God is born within us.

When we talk about the Incarnation, we talk about God becoming human through Jesus. We fail to take the idea of the Incarnation further: God becoming human through us. We have isolated Jesus, stuck him in a box and mounted it on a pillar. And we say God became human in Jesus as if that is the end of the story—God is finished.

God never finishes. God is a constant birther, continually revealing God's presence to those whose hearts and minds are open.

People are hungry and grasping for the divine, but we do not imagine the divine is hidden within us, as well as being soaked in the universe. We have removed ourselves from our own beauty. We are so used to looking for holiness outside of the human and outside our own reality that we have lost our inner sense of beauty and our awe at the mystery of God in all things.

The mystics remind us that God is in all things. Meister Eckhart said:

> Apprehend God in all things, for God is in all things. Every single creature is full of God and is a book about God. If I spend time with the tiniest creature—even a caterpillar—I would never have to prepare a sermon. So full of God is every creature. [1]

Everything is, because God created. Our task is to recognize God already present and to bring to the surface God's presence through our faith, our belief. If we truly believe that God created this Earth and God created all that is on the Earth then we realize that we are walking on sacred ground and that we ourselves are sacred.

Native American cultures and other tribal peoples have no difficulties with this. They recognize the Earth as sacred, they honor nature. They see God in our environment and recognize that God reflects everything and God is present in everything. They do not isolate God. They believe God's life throbs in everything.

If we truly understood and believed that, we would not pollute our world or our bodies. We would not pour toxic waste into the Earth that God birthed, we would not pollute the air that we breathe for it is also God's breath.

We move from speaking with and at God, to experiencing God in all things. We carry God with us all the time. Teresa of Avila gave us this image of God:

> God is as rain falling into the waters of a river. The rain cannot be divided from the river. Neither can we be separated from God. [2]

---

1. Matthew Fox, Meditations With Meister Eckhart, Bear & Co. 1983
2. Campbell, Meditations with Teresa of Avila, Bear & Co. 1985

Meister Eckhart said,

> The seed of God is in us. Now the seed of a pear tree grows into a pear tree; and a hazel seed grows into a hazel tree; a seed of God grows into God.

If indeed there is a seed of God in each of us, I believe that we are out of touch with it. We don't nurture it, we don't give birth to God. If we are truly aware that God is breathing deeply within our humanity, (I say, about three inches in from the belly-button,) and if we nurture that life, we can be transformed.

We are capable of becoming impregnated with God within our whole life if we recognize and acknowledge God's presence and embrace it. God will become in us when that happens.

Our very awareness of God within is our prayer. That is the mystical experience. God is there and we feel awe and amazement, though we are not always conscious of it. It is like background music, it is there and we become aware of it whenever we fall into a state of deep consciousness.

Even when we get stuck in stuff and get caught up in activities God is always within us. Instead of reaching out to God, we have to learn to sink within. Good works and public worship give us a sense of security because we can consciously control, and be seen to be active, whereas sinking within is hard to validate. Who is going to tell us whether we are sinking deep enough or far enough? We are like children, we want someone to guide us, see us, applaud us. But no-one can see within us.

When we accept that each of us is endowed with the divine presence and is capable of sinking into it, following the footsteps of Jesus, then we realize that we do not always need the mediators of the divine that we have created and come to depend upon. The priests, priestesses and shamans are merely stepping-stones laid before us in the direction of the divine. It is not their authority or creeds to which we must be converted, but rather to the amazing reality of God breathing deeply within our own little selves.

§

We have more serious business to be about than asking God to win the baseball match or do this or that favor for us. The life of prayer is not a party or a flea market where we rummage for goodies. We need to realize that God loves us and will provide for us whether we ask or not. In the Christian scripture we read:

> Jesus said, 'in truth I tell you, there is no one who has left house, brothers, sisters, mother father, children or land for my sake and for the sake of the gospel who will not receive a hundred times as much...
> MARK 10:29-30 NJB

We need to grow up and stop asking God for presents and party favors.

I lived for a nine months in a hermitage. Essentially it was a time when I was asking God to show me direction. I was writing down things and going over pros and cons. We grow up with a structure and sometimes we need to use the structure as a ladder. It is part of what makes us human that sometimes we must deliberately organize our thoughts and needs and prioritize them. I think God watches and smiles at our efforts.

Everyone is running around desperately looking for pointers and clues that will tell us which way to go. What kind of a God is it that we imagine says, "I have a great plans for you but I guess you are going to have to work really hard to find out what they are?" It would be like a mother with a child and the mother saying, "I have secret desires for you, my child, but you must find out what they are and one day you will hit the jackpot and you'll know what I want for you." A mother doesn't do that. My son, Niall, says to me, "Mama, what do you want me to be when I grow up?" I say, "Whatever will bring you the greatest joy and peace." He says, "Yes, Mama, but would you like me to fly a jet airplane or a puddle-jumper airplane when I'm a big man?" He wants me to say, "Do A,B,C and D," but he is beginning to understand that maybe I just want him to be happy and to be fulfilled.

It is the same with God. There is no treasure hunt no divine Olympics. We create these obstacles in our insecurity. We want someone to tell us exactly what God wants us to do. We want something concrete to focus on. Then we would have a task. We could read books about it. But if life is wide open, we have to fall into our dreams and discover our own joy in life. That is what God desires—our joy.

To take hold of this idea is frightening because it treats us as adults, not children who have to be told by parents what to do. We need only be aware of *God with us*. That awareness is our prayer and ultimately our path.

In prayer, as we become conscious of God, we become conscious of what it is we are called to do. The degree to which we are conscious of God's presence is the degree to which we will understand what we are to do with our lives. God cooperates on the journey, God plays with us and dreams with us and desires with us. God longs with us until we achieve our dreams, then God rejoices with us. God is also a child.

Passion

The Edge

It is safe by the edge
where the curling foam
falls into tiny bubbles.
Here I can walk
undisturbed by the depths,
unafraid of sinking
and dark silences.
Here, by the edge,
I can dance and sport,
leaving in the salt sand
slight indents
where my feet barely touched.
Here, by the edge,
I can quietly watch,
musing only
on how it must be
to be seized and swept
by the deep embrace
ever calling my name.

PASSION IS THE INEVITABLE consequence of our awareness of love. Once we awaken to God deep within us, we are overwhelmed. God is so close that we cannot but be filled with passion. It is hard to believe that God invites us to be so intimate. Like a dam bursting, this passion spills over into our relationships with others. It affects everything we do and everything we are.

When it is passion that drives us to do and be, the impact is greater than when we only think and plan on a rational level. Most of the work of transformation, that which endures and is most profound, is the result of passion. Much of the work I have done on the streets, or with the Volunteer Missionary Movement, or Genesis House, or some of the poetry I've written—where the experience has been profound—was born of passion.

We make an impact on our world when we have a deep awareness of God's grace in our lives. It is like having a well that we are able to draw from. The deeper it is, the more profound the consequences in terms of how we touch others and how our own lives are transformed.

Some would say that awareness of God deep within us is a consequence of the conversion experience which can come about when we are completely broken. Most of us live on a superficial level. We are forever treading water rather than sinking into the depths that are accessible to us. We do things in a shallow way instead of entering deeply into the wonder of life. Often a crisis or an experience of deep pain helps lead us to God who dwells in our deep places.

The mystics say that *attentiveness* is the most important aspect of holiness. In other words, when we are *aware* we are awake. The implication is that most of us are asleep half of the time. We are not picking up the miracles around us. We are not tuned in to the God life and the God grace in our selves, our environment and in other people.

To live on a deep level we need to sink. If we allow ourselves to sink, we lose control and sometimes it becomes very dark. We go down into a deep experience of joy, or pain, awareness, or grief. We don't see— we've lost our sight—but we *feel* deeply the experience.

We need to be much more aware of our gut feelings The mystical experience has to do with being at a gut-level. The mystic lives deeply and that requires a breaking down of all that makes us superficially secure. We have no control over emotions, over deep feelings, and we must allow God to carry us in our struggle, pain, dreams, and desires. It is *experiencing* life rather that a detached observation of life. When we plunge into life with a vigorous passion we may get our hands dirty and we may get hurt, but at least we are alive, and life cannot pass us by.

The saints and the mystics were profoundly alive— in touch with God in life and life in God. They lived at a very deep level. We must become such passionate, deeply-living people, even in a society where there is a dearth of passion and the constant buzz of superficial, passing pleasures.

Passion is born in us when we allow ourselves to be so loved by God that we cannot contain that love within ourselves. I experienced that when I was called to work on the streets of Chicago. Nobody in their right mind would sit down and say, "I think I will go into the inner-city where people are shooting, raping and mugging each other. I will walk around and say hello to the ladies in prostitution." That is not a rational academic's approach.

I fell in love with God again in an experience of prayer and solitude which stretched me to a deep awareness of God's love. And in that experience was the grace of stretching awareness. I knew through that experience that I was capable of doing far more than I ever imagined.

Passion can move mountains and have us walking on water—stuff we read and preach and pray about, but which we really do not believe or live out. You are authentic when you are no longer playing word games with God.

When we do say Yes to love, it is like plugging into an electrical socket. The current flows. We have created the conditions for that electrical current to go to work. We create the conditions for that jolt of fire in our gut. Then we know the risks we take are of no consequence. We will survive and be graced because we have connected to energy deeper than we normally access: God's grace and power. On a rational level we are familiar with the simile—we plug in, switch on and press buttons and things start happening. On the soul level we are even more capable of plugging in, making the circuit, and performing wonders.

We fall into passion by creating the environment of expectancy. We can compare falling into passion to giving birth. We have to be expectant of the possibilities of God's miracles. We have to be capable of giving birth to God, surfacing God's presence. When we have created a womb-like environment deep within us, God's seed can be nurtured by our small faith. God does not require a lot to transform our lives.

We are not here to sit and receive God's gifts, passive recipients of some Santa Claus, we are here to cooperate in miracle work and in transformation! That means we are involved, we are co-creators with God. God is always hungry and longs to be born and surface in our world, but cannot, does not, unless we cooperate and say *Yes.* Yes to the great pregnancy. In Christian tradition we get the great Yes of Mary. Would she give birth to the child of God? Yes! Mary did not hang her head and murmur "Okay, whatever you say..." Our response must not be a passive thing, but a resounding Yes! I believe, and I am open to God's transforming grace. We need to get pregnant with the divine. Meister Eckhart said we are all called to be mothers of God.[1] No small task, but perfectly feasible.

§

We are all capable of passion but we are embarrassed by it because it is so unpredictable and overcomes our ability to keep rational control. We like to discuss and debate—let's sit down and get the facts and figures, let's line up everything in proper order. God forbid that we should allow our hearts to go before us! We have to stop putting our brains first and we have got to begin to put our hearts first and become a compassionate people.

Instead of saying, "Wait a minute how much are we going to make? Is it going to be to our benefit? And will we be secure and safe?" we have to say, "What is the most loving thing to do?" If we put our hearts first we would, little by little, heal our world—and ourselves in the process.

---

[1] Matthew Fox, Meditations With Meister Eckhart, Bear & Co. 1983

When we are passionate we take risks—and who wants to take risks? Most of the time we sit out on the periphery of life, asking if we are going to be alright. But our spiritual tradition is a risk-taking tradition. Jesus took risks. Gandhi took risks, as all great leaders take risks for justice. Our stories show us that those who are most honored and made the greatest impact in our world were risk-takers.

God gave us this world, created this world and told us to look after it, take care of it—what an incredible risk that was! And of course we are not taking care of it, with our polluting and bombing and raping and destroying and fighting. I think we are beginning to realize that if we are to survive, we must remember and honor the original call to love one another and to be stewards of this Earth. It is passionate love which will impel us to honor and care for Earth rather than mastering and controlling and oppressing it.

Jesus came to set fire to the Earth, and how he wished it were burning already! Jesus was very hot, Jesus was very passionate. He lived passion. He loved people, he loved the little ones, he received the beggars, he received the women. In the temple he became incensed with the moneylenders. He lived in passion and he died in passion, and that is why he made such an impact on history.

Jesus was attuned to the Holy Spirit. The fiery breath. The Holy Spirit is the feminine dimension of the Trinity. The Holy Spirit is also free—the one who wanders around. She is the one we cannot contain or control but to whom we must be open so that we might be transformed.

We can and have put .God in a box, we have put God as Father in a box, we have put the Son in a box, but not the Holy Spirit. She wanders around looking for open hearts to convert and to receive her. She is the birther, she is the one who will bring about new things if we are open to her fire. Fire and passion are linked. We often get embarrassed when we talk about fire and passion and feeling, and we either dismiss them as unimportant, or they affect us for the rest of our lives. We have a choice: we either enter deeply into transforming passion or we take the fire out of these very sacred experiences and become all dried up ourselves.

God is always waiting for us with longing and passion. We are the ones who can choose to sink into God's grace and God's presence. It is our readiness and openness to the experience which is critical if we are truly to fall into God. That is the kind of power God has given us. Yet we are reluctant to claim this power because we have created a distant God who, we imagine, decides whether or not to visit us and fill us with grace and holiness. In other words, we have abandoned our great potential for union with the divine by pushing the initiative onto God. People say, "I could never be holy, God doesn't listen to me." We should say instead, "Of course I am called to the stars, of course I am called to be a mystic."

A child never really thinks about the mother's responsibility but knows the mother is there for her and will always take care of her. The child is not constantly concerned with how she can please her mother, unless there is some sort of unhealthy relationship. Children don't do that unless there is a problem in the relationship. We do it with God because there is a problem in our relationship. We do not understand how much of a lover and a mother God is. If we did understand we would know that we do not need to plead and beg of our Mother.

We must take God for granted. We must know that God is ever there, before us, behind us, around us. Awe is born of such an awareness. Like the all-embracing love of a child for her mother, it is awesome. Maybe this is too much for us to handle, and why we do not enter deeply enough into the love, to be bowled over by the enormity of God's great compassion for us.

If we knew it, if we experienced even a little of it, we ourselves would be lovers. We would be lovers of each other. We would be lovers of nature. We would go around with our eyes shining with passion because we would be touched by the divine. We would *know* God is Love.

Self Esteem

I am Your Dream

I am your dream,
I swell your soul
in a moment of suspended grace.

I am your dream
I dance on waters shining
in the rising sun.

I am your dream –
diamond glinting –
in night's display of stars.

I am your dream,
I hide in you –
burning in your deeps.

I am your dream –
your breath of God –
waiting to be born.

A LOT OF PEOPLE THINK THAT they will become holy by
going outside themselves and relating to some divine
'Other.' My understanding of my own spirituality and
that of others in the Christian and mystical tradition is
that we reflect God's grace from our deep human reality,
from who we really are. Unless we come to love ourselves,
unless we come to recognize God in our humanity, we
will not deeply experience God. Many people are broken,
have very little self-esteem and are subject to all kinds
of addictions because they do not accept themselves or
have not dealt with their personal problems. As much as
we reject ourselves, we reject God, for we are made in
God's image, we are God's work of art. If we cannot
handle being God's work of art, if we cannot accept that
we are the temple of the Holy Spirit then how are we to
find God anywhere else?

The process of healing is vital to becoming holy. We
have to come to so love ourselves that we discover at the
depth of all our turmoil God inextricably living in us.
We throw God away when we throw ourselves away,
when we cannot embrace ourselves.

We must start with ourselves, not God. God is the end
point. We embrace ourselves, our bumps our lumps our
lovely bits, our mucky bits—loving everything into
healing, wholeness, loving ourselves into a joy-filled
people. And then our eyes will reflect the discovery of
God's grace within ourselves. You know truly holy
people by looking at *them,* not the crucifix they may be
holding nor by seeing them kneeling and making holy
gestures. You know they are holy by the light coming out
of their eyes. You have only to look at someone like the
Dalai Lama or Archbishop Desmond Tutu or Mother
Teresa to know this. Such people shine with the love of

God. There is something about their whole being that we want to embrace. It is because they have come to understand that God is within them. And because of that awareness they allow God's light to shine through their eyes. It affects the world around us when God's love shines from our eyes.

But if we hate ourselves, abuse ourselves or hurt our bodies with drugs or alcohol—however we choose to hurt ourselves, we diminish God within us. It is the same when we pour toxic waste into the Earth and slash and burn God's creation, we harm the Earth, we harm ourselves. The journey of a holy people is one where we will come to sacralize the world and ourselves by recognizing these are God. When we walk in a sanctuary or enter a synagogue, any holy place, we are conscious of being on holy ground. We need to do that everywhere. Imagine what our world would look like if we treated all of it in this way. Imagine if we treated one another as sacred vessels of God's grace, God's seed. We would not be able to kill one another. We would be incapable of raping because we would know we would be raping or destroying something of God. And that is the consciousness to which this generation is being called.

A new spiritual consciousness, a new spiritual awareness is breaking through. A few people are starting to stumble upon the sacredness of life. We are old, young, black, brown, and we are beginning to embrace a new way. We are beginning to take care of the Earth, knowing that it is integral to who we are. We are beginning to see that we are all connected—that we are all part of one another and part of this Earth, and we must recognize and honor our one-ness. And that is what holiness is about. So we must fall in love with our world and ourselves and fall in love with God in the process. Then, inevitably, we will love one another.

When we allow other people to tell us who and how we should be—you must be thin, beautiful, you must wear this, think that—we are far from God. When we allow others to become our little gods rather than allowing God to shine through us in exactly the way we are made, we have become dependent on external forces, the agencies and corporations that simply want us to spend money and in the process adopt their images and likenesses. Thus we void our self-esteem. Thus we sell ourselves.

The consumer gods come and say, "This is how you must look," and because of our neediness and our insecurities we begin to follow them like sheep. Sheep! We all flock together and trade our power, our potential divinity for goods and commodities that we imagine make us more acceptable.

But we are slaves, bonded to commercial corporations. We are bonded to those who would run and buy and sell our lives. So we lose our own selves. If we lose ourselves we have nothing. And we *feel* we have nothing, but we still keep on this mad, mad path, looking for meaning outside ourselves instead of finding it deep within us.

The women in prostitution have taught me this. Their lives are devoted to making themselves marketable and selling themselves. I don't know a prostitute who has self-esteem. I don't know any woman in prostitution who is able to say truly, "I love myself," until they are well on their way to recovery. On the contrary, they say, "I am nothing, I am nobody, I hate myself." And then they compound that hate with street drugs and alcohol because they don't want to be aware of their bodies or themselves. So they sell themselves out of existence. But deep within there is still the God seed which calls them constantly back home to themselves and to the God within them. There will be such a homecoming, such celebration!

This is the story of the Prodigal Son in the New Testament. The young man says that in order to really live, to prove his existence, he must go out, spend money, win friends and applause. He comes to realize that the life he has chosen is empty and he is called back to God when he reaches the depths of despair and asks himself what he has really gained. It is a moment of conversion. So it is with recovery from addictions, and all things that tie us down. We know when we have hit bottom when we find we have the most beautiful clothes, the most wonderful hairdo, the food, the house, the cars. But inside we feel empty and irrelevant. None of this is ever going to be enough. The only thing that will fill our hunger is God.

And it is God who will carry us. Real fulfillment has nothing to do with commerce and ownership of property and exercised power. Real fulfillment has to do with embracing one's own inner potential. When we do that we can work miracles!

This is the process I see in women in recovery. Take Linda—of all the women I encountered on the streets, she was the most lost. She hated herself. But now her eyes shine and her voice is magical. She had been dead in the darkness of the tomb, living a life-style of drugs and prostitution. But one day the stone was rolled away and she saw the light, realized that she could walk, and came out into a new life, throwing off everything that she had in death, like a butterfly emerging from its cocoon. Now she witnesses to God by her shining life. In order to come to that new life, Linda had to hit bottom as she did and come to find God still alive and passionate within her. She let go of the old life and in the emptiness that followed resurrection took place.

We need to embrace our humanity, no matter how bruised or battered it is. We must die to our pride—our egos which tell us we are quite good enough. We must believe, no matter how many our failings or how deep our shadows and neuroses, that God holds us in the palm of God's hand, gazing on us with joy, dreaming of our wondrous possibilities and waiting with longing for the moment when we recognize our infinite potential.

Dying to enter into new life is a classical spiritual theme. Think of the phoenix that feeds her young on her own blood, think of the fertility rites that celebrated the end of winter and the coming of spring, and, of course the seed that must die to bring forth new life. But our generation, and particularly North Americans will do anything to avoid death. We will put you on an intravenous drip, we will hook you up and keep your heart beating, we will make you into a machine, but we will not let you die. We feel we have to extend life no matter how poor its quality, as if death is some awful thing to be forever kept at bay. We do not want to die. But we must.

Spiritually, death is life, it leads to life. And even physically, for those who believe in God or the mystery of eternal life, death is also the beginning. So why we should be so resistant to dying spiritually, dying to our desires, and dying to our images is amazing. Death is so much part of our human story. We need to embrace death.

True wholeness comes only when we are able to look deep within and say, "This is who I am called to be." We are the way God has made us, in God's image and likeness. And as we accept that and stand with dignity and joy in that reality, the more we experience true freedom.

Mothering

Mothering

So soft and fresh you burst, my son
from the darkness of creation—
all curled up and embryonic
you came to meet the world.
And I watched you unfold
like a breaking seed spilling out,
as you explored
every waiting space,
meeting with awed gaze
the cracks and holes and bits of fluff
you encountered on the ground
on which you sucked and crawled.
Like a timid goddess—
honored, but intent on co-creation,
I nurtured you
through nights and days,
coaxing your beauty
to shine in our grey world,
proud of your growing strength
and amazed at your simple wisdom—
bemused by the heavy, complex ways
of grown ups.
You reminded me, son,
of how old we have become,
and how we have traded delight and play
for stocks and shares and security.
But at night,
all noise and laughter stilled,
I watch you, tightly curled—
your dreams not yet sprung
upon the Earth,
and I listen to your steady breathing
as I sing my lullabies
in the darkness,
dreaming with you,
sweet son,
of a fresh and new-made world
wrapped up,
like you,
in rainbows.

BEFORE I BECAME A MOTHER I was a free spirit, able to do many apparently wonderful things. People would say how marvelous it was to go off to Africa to be a missionary and work with the poor and build a school, and then to go to Chicago and work with the women on the streets. People have great admiration for such callings and think you admirable if you undertake them. When I had no other commitment I spent months in hermitages in the desert and later in a trailer in the woods.

I was able to follow my heart, follow the Spirit. Then, when I hit fifty, I adopted a newborn child and everything else came to a full stop. You cannot suddenly go hiking off into the desert or the forest to pray and commune with the infinite when there are diapers to change and formula to buy and sticky fingers to clean up.

Motherhood has been a true learning experience for me. It has bought me down from the mountain top, in from the desert and to the kitchen and the bathroom. Most people are trying to get out of the kitchen, and here I was in my middle years, domesticated, singing my little baby to sleep night after night after night, and I am still doing it seven years later.

I have been led to discover that we are to sanctify all we do. No human experience is to be given a special status over another. Being a missionary or a desert hermit might appear more dramatic than looking after a baby, but appearances are deceiving. It is how we live life that is important. It is not what we do or what we achieve that is significant, but *how* we do it. To feed a baby can be as sacred as sitting on a mountain and singing holy songs. I think I needed to know that, I needed a dose of everyday reality. The experience of caring for a young one helps me understand that God is everywhere.

If I am really honest, bringing up a child has been a far greater challenge than founding the Volunteer Missionary Movement, or anything else I have accomplished. Being a mom, so far, has taken more commitment, energy and devotion than trying to change the world! Ironically parenting is something we often discount as unimportant: it is nothing special, nothing to do with being a saint or being spiritual.

I have learned that we must rediscover the inherent call to wholeness in the experience of being a mother or a father. When I find myself missing my desert and my mountain tops I have to be brought back to earth and realize that my son's smiles and tears and games and little crises are as significant as the big revelations or insights in the overall plan of things.

Motherhood has also helped me to be more 'real' in responding to people when I am leading a retreat or giving an address. Some of them tend to put me on a pedestal, they think I have achieved great things and wait with bated breath for what Edwina is going to be doing next. Is she opening a home for the brokenhearted or for Kosovo refugees? And I say, "Well, actually I am bringing up a child." Then there is a hesitation, and the question again: "But what are you *doing?* And that says a lot about our society and how we have lost the inherent value and importance of nurturing our children, and what it means to be commissioned to co-create with God. I am aware that my child will reflect what I have given him, and that through God's grace this is my particular contribution to the human race. It is astonishing to have a human soul in your care, to know that to a great extent you influence who he becomes. Being a mother is a sacred task. It has taught me that creating and deepening a relationship demands holiness. Reaching out to others is spiritual work. So while going off alone and being a hermit may be important, it is certainly no more wonderful than singing my child to sleep up in the bedroom.

Holding Niall and loving him and protecting him, I get a glimpse of how God must feel for us. If we understand that our love is much more limited than God's love, how powerful God's love must be!

I have found that our natural surroundings is a good place to start teaching my child about God. This is what God made for us to live in, our Garden of Eden. If my son can come to see and experience God in every living creature, not only in himself but in the birds and every animal and the trees and the Earth and all that grows and lives, then he will realize that he is part of an incredible network of sacred connections: that his is also part of God's body and everything that lives and breathes is part of God.

So it is important to me to teach my son spirituality instead of religion—that God is bigger than our religious traditions, our inadequate attempts to try to contain and explain the divine. We need only to run out into the meadow or walk in the forest to glimpse the divine. And a sense of awe is critical to divine consciousness. Awe of the Divine, awe of Creation around us. Children are naturally awed, though we start to knock it out of them before they go to school and sadly, by their early teens it's pretty well gone. Children are born with wonder, they are born, as the poet Wordsworth said, *trailing clouds of glory from God who is their home.*

The other day I was upstairs with Niall and he was crying as I was putting him to bed. I think he was upset by some story he had heard, or something he had seen on the television. Anyway, he was sobbing and sobbing, so I asked him why. He said, "Mama, I want to go back to where I come from. I want to go back to God because God isn't scary and the world is scary so I want to go back now!" It was one of those statements that children come out with which blow your mind. This child absolutely wanted to go home to God, because what he had seen had frightened him, but he had an awareness that God is home, that God is love. From that perspective I felt deeply comforted that I had taught him that God will always be there for him, that God will be home for him and that is where he came from.

I teach Niall to talk to God every night when I take him to bed. I always pray, and I say things like, "Didn't you have fun diving in the pool to day? Thank you, God, for water. Thank you for swimming, for legs." So whatever he has done in the day I make into a prayer and connect it with God. And then I ask if there is anything he would like to pray about, and sometimes he says he is praying in his heart.

Sometime Niall comes up with the most beautiful spontaneous prayer. Kids do. If children develop an ability to chat to God, they will make friends with God. Niall talks to his toys, his model airplanes, his stuffed animals, and it is important that he talks to God too. At this point they are probably all mixed-up together: a jet plane may be as important to Niall as God, which is fine. It's important that he knows God is central in my life and special in my life.

He knows that whenever we go walking we always come up with something about God: "Look what God did there! Look at that spider, didn't God do a good job?—Hey, Mama, God did a really good job with that one, didn't she?"

He thinks God is a mother, a big brown person in heaven. We all go through spiritual stages and it is important to be aware of your children's own images of God. God will be a daddy or a Mama who gives presents, and that is fine. But we must not stay with an infant's idea of God, eventually we must embrace a more adult version. Niall has taught me, and reminds me all the time, that we are never to reject anyone's religious experience. You know, when suddenly it's all Zen, or suddenly this tradition is in, or that tradition is out—and so why are you still in the Church? The arrogance of being fashionable! The arrogance that says, "This is the truth and this is the only truth, and I have got it." As long as we faithfully continue the journey towards deepening our understanding of God, who can speak against us?

There are certain stages which it is very important to go through. If I had not gone to church and said the rosary and gone to benediction and confession, I probably would not have had a foundation which was secure enough to fly from into a darker place. So I think we have to meet children where they are in their knowledge of God, and understand the significance of their being able to look at a butterfly with awe. Everything is useful to the spiritual journey, nothing should be discarded lightly. The problem is, we get stuck with images that have served their purpose, things that no longer speak to our experience, and we keep carrying them with us for security reasons. The spiritual pursuit is a journey which does not stop in one place, it must forever change, but every part of it from beginning to end is significant.

The degree to which we are open to the different experiences that God provides is often the degree to which we will be stretched. As for me, a white Englishwoman, adopting Niall, an African American boy, I really thought I was liberated enough to be able to do it without skipping a beat. But I think my son has stretched me further into being much more committed to struggle against racism. When you love somebody as much as I love my little brown son, you have to oppose any kind of barrier that keeps people from being one with each other, from being brothers and sisters. Being Niall's mother has lit in me a deeper passion for justice and equality. We put ourselves on the line when we love. Love leads us to be prepared to give our own life for the sake of it. And we realize that no one is to be excluded, no one is to be discounted, whatever their culture or nationality, race or religion. What is important is that within each one of us God's seed lives.

My love for my child is constant. I have loved other people and then moved on, but you could never do that with a child. They are with us forever. God loves us too, with constancy and commitment. Motherhood has taught me that.

So it is with God's grace. It is constant, no matter how much we do wrong. God is hungry for us, lonely without us. We are the ones who do not see that God is close as a shadow. God walks with us as a mother. I know how important it is for me to walk with my son, and I know in one way or another I will be with him until I die. I cannot imagine life without my child, even as he grows up and becomes less dependent on me. I will always care for him, be anxious for him. Now God is much more than that for us, and if we can consider a mother's love as a faint reflection of God's love for us, we will realize that we don't have to do anything except live our lives as fully and as well as possible, and God is there waiting for us with open arms, all the time.

We try everything to catch God's attention without realizing that it never wavered from the very beginning. God never stopped gazing upon us. What we have to do is recognize that gaze rather than seek God's attention.

Just as good parents would never dream of letting their children wander off, God is as careful with us throughout our lives—even in our anxious old age. God is in love with us. Anxiety is one of the greatest deterrents to spiritual peace, it is born of our lack of trust in God. That is why we relentlessly seek God's attention, we seem to believe that unless we plead and pester, God will ignore us. As if a mother would do that.

Stretching

Stretching

Small we are born,
curled up,
then kicking,
delighting in the stretch
and the surge of life
as tiny limbs thrust against the air,
knowing freedom.
But we grow,
and we become
more cautious
in our dance
lest we stumble,
or, careering in emptiness,
we fear there is none
to break our fall.
But if we dare remember
the joy
that once we knew,
the spontaneous leaps
of childhood
and reckless climbing
to the stars,
we might capture again
that free wild Spirit
waiting to leap
into opened hearts
to propel us,
whirling in God's breath
far beyond
those childhood stars.

MINISTRY CONSISTS IN REACHING OUT. It starts with nourishing one's own inner life so that we can share God's grace with others. The work I have done both in Africa and in Chicago has been for my own conversion and spiritual health as much as for anyone else's. Some people will take this as a humble reply to their saying how wonderful it must be to work with women in prostitution, or to teach in poverty-stricken African villages. The truth is, I don't think I had much of a say in the matter. I think God propelled me into those African villages and the inner-city for my own growth. We often imagine that we are here to save the world, to heal people, that we are here to do any number of marvelous things, but first and last we are here to grow into the fullness of God's presence, and that can be done only in relation to other people.

We cannot separate other people from our own becoming. I have learned more from African people and from women in prostitution than ever I could have taught them. They have been my gift. I think in our arrogance, we so-called ministers may imagine that we are God's gift to the world, God's gift to the poor, and we can miss the fact that the poor are God's gift to us. The poor know what life is like when it is stripped down to basics: no masks, no sophisticated game-playing. I have experienced the authenticity of their spontaneous embrace, and that turned my first idea of ministry upside down.

We ministers and missionaries, are the ones called to conversion—as we summon the faith to get close to the poor and the brokenhearted. It is not something we do easily because it can break our hearts. It certainly broke my heart to experience what people on the street must endure, but eventually their love healed me. A hard heart

72

needs to be broken open. Those who we most readily reject are those who we most need to be with. To say this now may sound glib, but it is true nonetheless. I know these women in prostitution have made me gentler, they have awakened a sensitivity in me which might never have surfaced had I not known them. It is clear to me that the more we are exposed to brokenness in this world, the more compassionate we become.

My ministry is not a matter of courage or bravery or wondrous achievement, it is a matter of being faithful. It is a matter of plodding along, doing what I am supposed to be doing. It is as simple as that.

Of course people want me to keep achieving what they perceive as wonderful things, but physically, mentally and spiritually it is hard to survive being out on the streets year after year. There are rhythms in life: we are called to go out and to get involved, and then we must withdraw, become renewed and refreshed. Maybe our calling changes. It is all part of life's changing journey. Perhaps we are sent into a particular situation to learn and to grow in a one direction, and then we might be called back by God's grace to develop another level of consciousness.

When people ask me if I am still working on the streets of Chicago, and I tell them that I am not, I am not working directly with the women in prostitution. I still spend time with the women (they are such a joy and inspiration to me), mostly I take them on retreats to country areas where they can experience and enjoy nature and the beauty of the open countryside. We pray and play and celebrate and dance together. We experience God. But mostly I do down-to-earth simple things like writing and giving retreats and bringing up my son. What we do is not important, but the love with which we do it.

What is perceived as my active ministry started off in Africa, and it was African people who first opened up my heart, and then the women in prostitution in Chicago stretched my heart further. After some years the time came to pull back from those experiences and reflect, and share in writing and speaking with a wider society what I had learned in Africa and on the Chicago streets. I know there is an urgent message in my experiences and my task is to communicate it. Though telling that message is not as dramatic as being in the bars at night or the brothels by day, it nevertheless has to be done.

Not everybody is called to work with people with drug addictions or the homeless, but all of us at some time need to expose ourselves to the pain of poverty—to stay in touch with it until it is no longer a reality. Whether it means we go down to the local soup kitchen once a week or we help at the Salvation Army hostel, all of us need to stretch, to push our boundaries.

We are all called to stretch in different directions. Some of us (like me) need more violent stretching than others. And what stretches us will be different for each of us. One may have five kids to bring up, another may have all kinds of broken-heartedness, or be battling cancer or drug addiction. Whatever the case, we must be open to the growth that these experiences offer us, and deepen in compassion towards others. What we must not do is hide ourselves in a little cocoon of security, lock ourselves in gated communities and say, "I don't want to know what anybody else is doing, I don't want to see anything unfamiliar, I don't want to push my boundaries," because then we shrivel up spiritually. We keep our juices flowing by being open to the human dynamic in all its pain and brokenness as well as in its beauty and joy.

There are many people who reject the opportunity to be stretched and therefore to get bigger in their hearts. They say, "I am not going to go near those people—they look different, they smell different," and that closes a door to God. God will take us to the edge of a cliff in order for us to experience miracles. Unless we are prepared to go to the edge of the cliff, we will not see the incredible view.

Reaching out is not a matter of *doing* for others, it is a matter of growing through others and with others. The Church had a very different understanding of mission in the past, and still today there are people in the Church and other institutions who believe we have to go out and convert people to our own image and likeness, rather than seeing in them God's reflection and so growing in our understanding of God.

I think when we expose ourselves to opportunity to grow and stretch, compassion comes along with it. We become compassionate when we see the brokenness of others and receive it in love. How else will we become saints, how else will we become holy unless it is through the brokenhearted?

Letting Go

Darkness

In this place
there are no whispers
to remind me of the living,
there is only a greyness
which does not breathe
nor move;
In this place
is the absence
of all that is familiar
and kind
of all that is warm
and tender.
Here,
in this place,
I meet death –
yet cannot die –
but am only an observer
of my own
disintegration.

THERE IS A TENDENCY TO IMAGINE that to be open to the spiritual journey must be a terribly serious business, all rather pious and ponderous. I think that God must have a great laugh seeing us going around with furrowed brows and getting into all sorts of anxious states in our pursuit of spirituality. But growing in the spiritual life is not a heavy affair, it should lighten our hearts and raise our spirits.

Julian of Norwich gained an insight when she had a vision of God in which God showed to her in the palm of her hand a small hazelnut. Julian asked what it meant, and came to understand that the hazelnut was to show how small and yet secure and loved we are, held in the palm of God's hand.[1] We must have that perspective. Since we are not the center of the universe, we do not need to take ourselves so terribly seriously. We lose track, we lose the meaning of wholeness when we do that.

One of the consequences of thinking that our small faith is of such importance is that we think everybody else needs it. And still, even in our time, we earnestly send out missionaries to convert people to our beliefs. And it is all dreadfully serious: terrible things might happen if one does not believe and does not go to church to pray just as we do. But God reveals God's self to people in myriad ways and when we try to possess and monopolize God, saying that our Church or our religious experience is the only one, we dismiss the richness and diversity of God's creation and revelation. We need to lighten up.

---

1. Julian of Norwich: Showings, trans. Colledge & Walsh, Mawah, Paulist Press, 1978.

We have spent hundreds of years dispensing our brand of God. We have gone up mountains and down dales all over the world, assuming the task of selling our boxed God to the world—as if it were our business! As if we had the responsibility of bringing God to humanity. God is already with humanity. God is already soaked in all human experience, our task is simply to be aware of the fact. Yet we have become dried up in our pious exercising and agonizing, we have even died for our absurd notions. Thank God that God escaped from our little packages!

Remember the story of the little fellow clattering through the city streets on his donkey? He's frantically galloping and everybody on the street asks him where he's going so fast? And he says, "I'm looking for my donkey!" And we are like that—so close to God that we miss God! We forget that we are already immersed in God, like a fish in water. We just need to relax and let go, to realize it.

For an example of how dried up and dull we have become, look at how the Church closed revelation in the year thirteen hundred, when it established the Canon of Scripture. That's it. The last holy book. The last revelation of God was in Jesus and that is *it*. God's story was cut off, finished. What happened to the idea that God is constantly, continually revealed through a forever changing humanity and universe? We are part of a story, we are part of an unfolding journey, and we are going to see different signposts and landmarks along the way. And we are going to say, "Oh look at that! *There's* a new revelation, a new understanding." So our awareness of God is deepened, expanded. And that's what should make the spiritual life exciting.

We who pursue the spiritual journey should be the most exciting, vibrant people on Earth. We should be bubbling over with the excitement of being pregnant, being potential birthers. The call to the journey never finishes. It is not as if we can say, "I've got it, I did it, I was there, I got God, here it is in this box." God grows with us and we grow with God. God is never final. In the Christian scriptures (Mark 8:17-19) we read, *Those who have eyes to see will see, those who have ears to hear will hear.* In this, I think Jesus was inviting us to recognize that God is indeed beyond our understanding and that we are tiny people. God holds us, a fragment of the cosmos, in the palm of God's hand. We are a miracle of God.

We don't know how big God is. We can hardly imagine life on another planet, let alone take care of the life on ours, and yet God extends throughout the billions of galaxies—and beyond. God is incomprehensible. All we can do is experience the energy in the universe, and that in a low-key way. People say Einstein used ten percent of his brain, and most people only use only five. We have hardly begun to develop! We are only just beginning to grow and to be aware of the divine, and we can only stand in awe that God's revelation is so rich and diverse. It is like a great banquet, forever waiting for us to taste. God is like a great banquet and we have only just begun with the hors d'ouevres. What a delight!

Psychologists say that one of the most healing things we can do is laugh. Given that we are called to wholeness, laughter must be integral to spiritual life and we need to bring humor and laughter into our worship, into our prayer.

Walk into any church service and we can pretty well guarantee we walk into what feels like a wake. We gather at the sanctuary looking grim, we gather around God's table to receive communion looking like we are going up to receive a bonk on the head rather than participate in the spiritual banquet. In conditioning ourselves to take God terribly seriously, confusing respect with a long face, we have missed out on the true meaning of God-with-us: Resurrection. *God is with us!* Jesus celebrated that with breaking through from death and the tomb. We must celebrate too, for resurrection means that even though we die we will live. We must let go of our fear.

Of course it is the noisy, excited children running down the aisles of the church who teach us this, the little children whom Jesus invited before him, because children have simplicity and openness. As we grow older we can become dull and boring and lose that spiritual joyfulness which children inherit from God and bring with them into their birth and infancy. And slowly we adults deprive them of their joy and freedom because it is all far too disorganized to fit neatly into our all-important boxes and categories.

By the time we get to middle age we may start looking again for that lost joy and freedom. Most of us just have to remember our childhood and learn to play, to run and dance, and we have to learn to laugh again. We will discover something of God in that freedom. But while we are serious, self-absorbed adults we feel silly doing those things. Spirituality *is* rather silly and we have to be rather silly to let go and allow ourselves to be children of God. Truly children of God.

The child of God knows that God is constant, and that the deeper one goes the deeper is the joy and the more profound the awe at God's presence in our lives. So surely we should be joyful, a people of hope, knowing that God will never leave us, but, little by little, according to our ability to see, will reveal to us the mystery and the wonder of God in us.

Plateaus

Plateau

It is this plateau –
now stretched nondescript and even
all around me –
which reveals
the rocky terrain and steeps
from which I came;
I see the sun
glinting on peaks
where once I stood –
awed at the heights
and the expanse around me.
And there,
falling behind me
in a great deep sweep,
I see the black chasms
of those dead places
where once I stumbled –
all broken up
and so alone.
Now there are no heights nor depths –
but only this vista
of wide open space,
revealing to me
the grace and courage
of faithful and brave journeying
which brought me here
to this piace
of steady, gentle breathing.

WE ARE HUNGRY FOR ICONS and heroines in our lives. I often find people looking to me, wanting to live vicariously my spirituality. I know others are subject to the same experience too. If I am on the streets of Chicago working with the women in prostitution and the drug addicts, some people feel gratified that somebody is doing, in their minds, the right thing. All well and good, perhaps, though nobody appears to be helped by this phenomenon, least of all the poor on the streets. For myself, I feel distinctly uncomfortable with being admired for simply following my heart. The truth is, I feel good when I'm doing something deemed worthy—we all feel good when we believe that we are helping others. We do not need to be dubbed heroes or heroines for responding to an irresistible call.

Those are peak moments in our lives, but the reality is we do not live on the peaks, we live mostly in the valleys. Yet people want their heroines and heroes to stay on the peaks and preach to them from up there, so that they can look up and be impressed. But we read in the Christian scriptures (Mark 9:2-9, Luke 9:28-36) where Jesus was on the mountain with his disciples; James, John and Peter, and there Elijah and Moses appeared to them in shining light and Jesus was transformed. The disciples all wanted to stay there, it was marvelous, they felt wonderful and Peter talked about putting up tents and staying in that great spiritual experience. Jesus' answer to this was a very clear admonishment to get down from the mountain. And there at the bottom of the mountain—not the top—the people were waiting, and Jesus did the work of healing the boy who was epileptic.

We are like Peter. We want our heroes and heroines to be doing wonderful things which make us feel good, but heroes spend most of their lives plodding along, sometimes bored, sometimes in quiet desperation, and often just longing for a little breakthrough. We must discover the spirituality and the beauty of plodding. We must focus on being faithful to the journey, and not allow ourselves to be tempted by mountaintops.

God is to be found in the mundane as much as at the mountain peak. God is to be found in tedium as much as in a glorious breakthrough. I constantly have to practice being aware of God in the everyday. I am not saving women in prostitution, I am not healing the sick, I am not clothing the naked. Instead, I may be sitting at home in the city with the kids running in and out, crying and screaming and throwing balls around, and I am making peanut-butter-and-jelly sandwiches. I have to experience the holy in that. I have to find God in the making of sandwiches.

So, everything is to be sanctified everything is to be made holy—including ourselves. In that process it is the ego that gets in the way—forever tempting us to trust and believe in our own power instead of allowing God's bright light to shine through us in all kinds of small and simple and ordinary ways.

Jesus is a great example of authentically seeking God in the ordinary. For two thousand years the memory of Jesus and the wisdom of Jesus has continued to fascinate the human race, yet only three of his thirty-three years were public. What made the three so dynamic, so important, were the previous thirty when he was simply working away as a carpenter, taking care of his mother and growing in his spiritual awareness.

We tend to disregard the content, we dismiss the foundational and we look for the frosting on the cake. Now, if there is no content, no foundation then the frosting will collapse. We are easily seduced by surface glamor and we fall into the trap of saying, "Oh because I am healing the sick, clothing the naked, performing grand works of mercy, I am closer to God." If we cannot be as close to God when we are sitting in our homes looking out of the window, then we have an unbalanced spirituality, we lack the foundation. We are building on sand.

We often associate spirituality and wholeness with fuzzy feelings or great miracles and breakthroughs. It is hard for us to think we are praying or that we are being faithful when we do not *tangibly* experience God's grace. I think a key to understanding authentic spirituality is knowing that it does not matter what we feel. It does not matter whether we are in a mystical trance or whether we are levitating or whether we are bored to tears. God is there—equally in all events, according to our openness of heart.

We cannot command God to give us a spiritual buzz by praying hard, or working hard on our inner growth, (though I think sometimes God has compassion on we poor humans and delivers the occasional bonus buzz). We must sit and receive God. We cannot procure, win, earn or bargain for God, though that way of thinking and instant gratification is what we are used to: a couple of keystrokes on the computer and the world is before us. We have an equation that runs our lives: hard work gets us money, money gets us our hearts' desire. There is nothing that we cannot obtain for ourselves, including, we think, God's grace—we know the right people, we are going to fly over and see the right guru... we are going to read all the right books. But none of that works with God. God will not be got. God is available to all from the poorest to the richest, but mostly to the simple souls who simply wait for God, believing that God is there. God will not be bought or bartered. Actually, we have to die in order to experience God, to die to the idea that we control our lives, and to die to what we appear to cherish most; our money, our lust for prepackaged sensual experience, our utter dependence on technology, our machinations to possess spirituality, to *own* —yes, even God,

To die to all this is the hardest thing for us to do. We can appreciate that the mystical experience requires letting go of much that we struggle daily to achieve, but we don't have the first notion of how we would function without our egos. So how do we teach people to let go? We can't. Each of us has to do it alone. One thing is clear: because God is to be found in the darkness, in the empty spaces, the more space we leave for God, the more God can be born within us. We who spend our lives acquiring things and property and bank balances are novices at letting go. The irony is that when we turn to someone else for guidance to the mystical, we may be only adding to the clutter.

Our journey is unique and ultimately it must be walked alone—much of it on plateaus and in valleys. Most of our lives we will not be working miracles, we will not be doing significant things. We will be plodding on, trying to get by, trying to be faithful.

I think that Jesus lived like that. The disciples thought Jesus was terrific because of his miracles. But when he was not working miracles and he was just hanging around being with the people, he was still authentically God's Son, as much as when he was feeding the five thousand and making the blind see. And he actually told his disciples that the miracles were insignificant, that they would do greater things. If we trust, if we believe, we will do greater things. Well, perhaps the greatest thing we have to do right now is to transform ourselves and our world by *doing* nothing, by simply *listening deeply* and waiting gently, planting ourselves firmly on our plateau without imagining we need to be scaling the next mountain.

If we are tuned in to the God within, we will know when we have to scale or move the next mountain. In the meantime we need simply to wait in attentive confidence.

Solitude

Invitation

I hover
between earth and heaven,
the one calling me ever outward
to whirl with the world
and lose myself
in myriad small doings and
momentous moments;
The other—
ah, the other,
gently disturbing and
ever whispering in
the hush of dusk or
stirring in night's silence,
inviting me
to wondrous Nothing,
there to sit alone
in solitude's gaping spaces,
awed,
at the nakedness of such a God.

EVERY NOW AND AGAIN in our whirlwind lives, we all experience the need to take a deep breath, to just pause a moment and get our bearings, to restore ourselves to the deep stillness that is in each of us. In doing this, from the spiritual perspective, we are called to sanctify our environment and to be a reflection of God in the marketplace, in the world and in society. We simply need to take a little space, however small. Length of time is not, important, it is the quality of the moment that counts. We withdraw to refocus ourselves and reroot ourselves in God's stillness.

This quiet pause is not, however, woven into the fabric of society, it is not something we honor. We do not honor silence, or those moments of being alone where the human spirit is given an opportunity to revive itself. Many people are well aware of this, we know that there is something missing, that there is a need for us to breathe deeply, but we do not know how to do it. And many equate time alone with being lonely.

There is a vast difference between being alone and being lonely. When we are lonely we feel isolated or disconnected. Being alone can be quite the opposite: it is a state in which we can feel connected to the deepest part of ourselves, to the deepest parts of life, when we become conscious of God within. We are not distracted, we do not allow ourselves to be wrenched in different directions by emotions and roller-coaster events. Withdrawing to be alone is restorative and sacred. It is almost a moment of going back to the womb, remembering where we come from and then being nourished by the life-giving juices of that experience.

Everything that I have done which I consider a breakthrough—like the foundation of the Volunteer Missionary Movement and Genesis House or going to Africa, these works have always been preceded by time alone with God. I am indeed hungry for such silent contemplation. Without the balance between the active and the contemplative, and silence and sound, we are unstable. We feel it, we know when we are out of balance, but often because we do not honor silence and space for ourselves, we do not permit ourselves to be blessed by quiet. As a consequence we do not learn to plumb our depths, and we live superficially. Peace eludes us.

I know that if I had not withdrawn I could not have heard the whispers in my soul that led me to important points in my life. Those whispers would have been drowned in the great volume of noise which accompanies our daily whirl of activity. To withdraw is an invitation to great blessing: to fall into our center and to be nourished by the richness there.

Solitude is not an escape nor the rejection of relationships, it thrusts us out into the world again where we are called to deepen our relationships and to sanctify the world. Of course we fear solitude at first, as we fear loneliness, we are so used to doing and talking that we can feel a sense of loss if we are purposefully nonproductive. We have such a need to prove, to justify our existence by showing what we have achieved, that actually *doing nothing* appears contrary to health and wellbeing! Yet we are all called to the solitude, like the plant that secretly grows downwards in the dark, moist earth and blooms only when it is well rooted. We all look for the fruit and flowers but there can be none without the roots and the accompanying silence and darkness.

There were times when I was alone in the forest that I felt God had left me. I do not think we can do anything about God seeming to abandon us. We do not have the authority to conjure up God's presence by saying, "Hey, come back, you've left me!" The only way we can endure or survive the emptiness when we suddenly feel that God has gone, is to *trust.* That is the moment of faith, it is a prerequisite for the experience of solitude. Such trust is especially difficult for a people accustomed to production on demand, whose wants are fed quickly by switching on the computer or by picking up the telephone. God is not an instant food. God is born slowly within us. And there in the midst of that quiet process we will most likely experience a sense of abandonment—a frustrating phenomenon, to say the least—yet it is to great purpose: for until we enter our own darkness we cannot be sensitive to the pain and brokenness of others.

As individuals, a microcosm of humanity, when we withdraw into solitude we experience all the abandonment and fear of the broken world. We experience all that within one human being, but we can hand it over to God. We do not try to change it, we do not try to control it, we simply sit in solitude with the pain. Ironically, in that passivity is empowerment. To sense that God is in charge, not us, is to find that we are finally able to approach the broken world without despair.

To find and practice solitude, we do not need to dramatically disappear to a hermitage for months on end, we can find it in little droplets—perhaps while waiting in line, for instance. Usually when we are waiting in line we are very impatient, because we are conditioned to instant gratification and response. But imagine, if we were so tuned in to the silence of God deep in our soul, that every time we found ourselves kicking our heels at the post-office or waiting at a red light, we took it as an opportunity for meditation—our lives would be transformed! With a little discipline, our lives could be impregnated with moments of solitude. If we consciously took such moments, however small, gradually we might develop the habit of being contemplative in every moment. The mystics and saints tell us we must live in the moment, that sanctity and spiritual fullness is all about *now,* this moment. This is our time of sanctification. It is not about yesterday. Whatever we did yesterday is over. Nor is it about the future: I am going to be holy, I am going to go be a hermit—that has not happened. The only thing we have is *now,* this moment. Whether you are waiting at the supermarket checkout, or lining up at the toll booth, that now is all we have.

I imagine that God sees just that. God is not concerned with what we have done and where we have been. God is so infinitely compassionate that God does not say, "Guess what, I have a punishment lined up for you, because remember what you did last year?" God does not do that. Instead God says, "Where are you now?"

The prophet Micah (7:19) talks about God throwing our sins to the bottom of the sea. That's where God wants them to be—unlike our society which seeks public retribution and vengeance. God has absolutely no interest in punishment. God is love. God is constantly forgiving us. What wrong we did two minutes ago is already forgiven. If we could enter into that awareness, of course we would be free people, we would walk around joy filled, because we would know that we are redeemed, we would know that we are resurrected. We cannot begin to imagine the depth and potential of God's compassion. When the realm of God breaks open, this is what it will be like: love will take over everything—like a mother with her child, endlessly loving, no matter what the child has done. I have seen mothers who sit with their children in jail, trying to hold their hands through the bars. The mothers know their children have done wrong and are being punished for it, but the mother loves utterly, she does not wish her child to be punished, all she knows is that this is her child before her. God is like that with us: "This is my child, you are mine and I love you forever, even to the gates of hell!" We might take God to the gates of hell but God will still love us and stand there with us.

We come to understand this impassioned love in solitude, because there we sink deep enough into God's presence to slowly become aware of God's embrace. The world will not tell us of that love, society will not tell us of that love, even the Church may not tell us of that love. But the mystics, those who have entered into God's presence, will tell us, because in solitude they have seen it.

People who answer the special calling to be contemplatives withdraw on behalf of the world, to be advocates for the world before God. Their response and their prayer and their sinking into God *does* make a difference. Like a pebble that falls into the water, their immersion in the divine somehow contributes to the sanctification of all of us. In times of crisis and suffering, think about how comforting it is to have someone we trust praying for us, focusing their thoughts on our problem and bringing those thoughts to God in silence. Somehow, in a way we cannot understand, that makes a difference. We are all connected. We affect one another whether we feel it or not. We are comforted and grateful when somebody is thinking of us or praying for us. So when contemplatives pray for the world, the world may not understand what they are doing, but something deeply spiritual does happen. And, of course, the contemplative prayer of any of us, for whatever period of time, affects the world too. We have not even begun to understand the effect that we can have on each other and on society when we pray, when we tap into the divine source within us and we project the healing grace from that source onto the brokenness of an individual or the brokenness of our world.

There is a place for everyone and when someone objects, "Just think what those contemplatives could be doing if they were out in the world, working with the poor," remember that there are already many working with the poor. It does not mean that everybody has to. We have to be faithful to our calling whether it is to be a carpenter, a doctor, a homemaker or a contemplative. Each is uniquely called to fulfill his or her gifts. The diversity of our gifts and vocations is wonderful. But all of us, at some time or other, are called to silent spaces. This call is not the prerogative of the consecrated or ordained—it whispers in the depths of every single one of us.

Taking care of ourselves involves our whole being: the spiritual, psychological, emotional and bodily aspects. We cannot pursue one and neglect the other without doing harm to the whole. We tend to focus on one aspect of our being to the detriment of the others. The great health fad in our society might be marvelous: everybody jogging and joining health clubs and eating their vegetables, but a bright, healthy body is a hollow shell if we neglect the spiritual or the psychological or the emotional.

Wellness means taking care of the whole person. The part of ourselves that is most neglected is the spiritual— because we are such sensual beings the physical demands attention first. We say, "I want to fix my hair, I want to look better, I want to feel better," so that is the first thing we do. It is okay to start there, but we must not stop there. There is a deep hunger in our soul. It cannot, will not be quieted. It is time for us to slow down, to let go, to find quiet, silent places, and to listen to the whispers. They will not go away—for God does not.

Jane and Edwina had a great time working together on this project.

Edwina is currently raising her son, but continues to write, speak and advocate for women in prostitution. She has journeyed far from her beginnings in Lancaster, England: living and working in East Africa, a hermitage, and on the streets of Chicago. She has a masters degree in theology and she is the founder of the Volunteer Missionary Movement and of Genesis House—a house of hospitality for women involved in prostitution. Her books are widely available.

Jane loves to travel, and lives in Southern California with her husband and two beautiful teenage daughters. She is a photographer and works from her in-home studio. She wears many hats but her favorite role is that of being a mom.